THE MOST
DANGEROUS JOBS
IN THE U.S.A.

JUNE A. ENGLISH

SCHOLASTIC INC.

New York • Toronto • London • Auckland • Sydney

To Bunky and Hoppalong

PHOTO CREDITS

Cover: top left: © Lewis/Liaison; top right: © Rob Johns/Liaison;
bottom right: courtesy of CDC; bottom left: © The Modesto Bee/Liaison.

Interior: 4 left and 24: © Benali-Gifford-Ferry/Liaison; 4 middle and 6: © The Modesto Bee/Liaison;
4 right and 35: © Rob Johns/Liaison International; 5: © Dennis Schroeder/Rocky Mountain News;
8: courtesy of Tiffan Thoele; 9, 10, 11, 12: © Superstock; 15: © Alain Buu/Gamma; 17 and 19:
courtesy of Kevin Chilton; 20: © Lewis/Liaison; 21: © Brad Lewis/Omjalla Images; 23: courtesy of
Steve McNutt; 25: © Leverett Bradley/FPG; 26: © Russ Kendall/Rocky Mountain News;
28: © Gail Williams; 30: and 33 courtesy of CDC; 31 and 32: © M. Schwarz/Gamma-Liaison;
36: © J. Pickerell/FPG; 38: © Andrew French.

Library of Congress Cataloging-in-Publication Data
English, June A.
The most dangerous jobs in the U.S.A. / by June A. English.
p.   cm.
Summary: Describes such dangerous jobs as smoke jumper, undercover cop, test pilot, and
epidemiologist and presents brief interviews with people who hold these risky jobs.
ISBN 0-590-89751-9
1. Hazardous occupations—United States—Juvenile literature.
2. Vocational guidance—United States—Juvenile literature. [1. Hazardous occupations. 2.
Occupations.] I. Title.
HD7262.5.U6E54   1998   97-26642
331.7'02—dc21   CIP
AC

12 11 10 9 8 7 6 5 4 3 2   02

Book design by Nancy Sabato

Printed in the U.S.A.   09
First printing, March 1998

Contents

Introduction

Lots of jobs are important. But some jobs are special—special because they're hard. And special because they're dangerous. This book is about some of the most dangerous jobs in the U.S.A. Some of them you might have guessed and some might surprise you. These jobs also have something else in common. They are jobs that serve people and keep them safe and protected. That makes these jobs not just dangerous, but really important.

Smoke Jumper

Smoke jumpers are a special kind of firefighter. They battle blazes in places that regular firefighters can't get to. Fires can start in the middle of a wilderness or on the side of a mountain. Firefighters can't drive to these places in a fire truck. So, smoke jumpers drop from an airplane close to the fire using parachutes. Dropping from a plane allows them to get to the fire area quickly. But parachuting into forest areas is tricky, especially near raging fires.

Sometimes smoke jumpers get hung up in a tree or smash into a boulder. Jumpers can easily break a leg or arm coming down to the ground. Wind gusts can land them in the wrong place. They may drop right into the middle of a fire. Occasionally parachutes fail. Then the jumper has to use her emergency chute to keep from crashing to the ground.

Smoke jumping is hard physical work. Jumpers have to be in top shape. Because they work in remote areas, they have to carry tools with them. These can include pickaxes, chain saws, and a digging tool called a pulaski. After fighting a fire, a smoke jumper has to hike out of the area. This can mean traveling miles with a hundred pounds of supplies on her back.

A smoke jumper's first job is to contain a fire. This means keeping it from spreading in an uncontrolled way. Firefighters do this by creating "lines" of fire. Sometimes they have to dig trenches or cut already burning trees. Clearing vegetation also keeps the fire from getting fuel.

Working around any kind of fire is dangerous. Tree fires are especially unpredictable. A super-heated tree can explode without warning. Burning trees can fall on firefighters, killing or injuring them.

Fires can also spread with lightning speed. Firefighters have to be sensitive to changes in the wind that can start cross fires. They have to notice changes in temperature. This could mean flames are moving their way.

Flames can spread around firefighters, trapping them in an inferno. So it's important that they figure out safe zones to work in. They need escape routes in case the fire becomes too fierce for them to stay.

Sometimes smoke jumpers can't escape from a blaze. So they have to try to survive inside it. They drop flat to the ground. Then they cover themselves with special flame-resistant blankets until the fire passes over them. This is a last resort, though. Only a lucky few will survive in the middle of a raging forest fire.

Smoke jumper Tiffan Thoele worked on a fire fighting crew for six seasons. Then she set her sights on becoming a smoke jumper. Working with her crew, she learned the basics of fire fighting; but becoming a smoke jumper took even more work. "Most of the training was physical," says Tiffan who lives in Oregon. "We learned how to jump out of a plane, how to do landing rolls, and how to get out of trees."

Tiffan also learned first aid and worked her way through a heavy-duty exercise program. Smoke jumpers also need a good basic education. But their instincts and drive are just as important. "A good firefighter needs to be able to think in stressful situations," says Tiffan. "And they need a little bit of healthy fear. Every fire has the potential to be harmful."

There are fewer than 400 smoke jumpers in the United States. Tiffan is glad that she's one of them. For her, the thrill of the job includes the great people she gets to work with. The beautiful natural scenery she sees also makes her job special. "Few people," says Tiffan, "get to do what I do and see what I see."

Undercover Cop

An undercover cop is an actor, a lawyer, and a police officer—all rolled into one. A detective who chooses undercover work has to be a jack-of-all-these-trades. And he has to keep all of them a careful secret.

Cops work undercover because certain cases demand secrecy. It's often much easier to catch a criminal when he or she doesn't know that a police officer is present.

Working undercover means you do the work of the police wearing street clothes instead of a uniform. Undercover cops pretend to be taxi

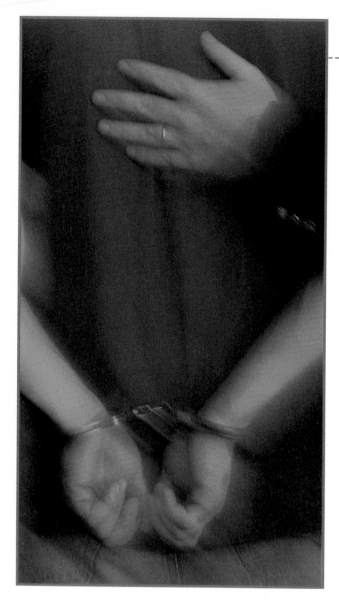

drivers, subway riders, homeless people, and even criminals. It's important that they aren't recognized. This may mean making their clothes look dirty or ragged. They may put on makeup to create a scar or even a different face. Good undercover cops have to be very convincing. They must almost become the person they are pretending to be.

People who do undercover work often get information from people on the street. These people are called informants. An undercover cop has to be able to find these people. He has to know which people to trust and which to avoid. Otherwise, the police could end up with the wrong information or the wrong suspect. The officer could even lose his cover and end up injured or even killed.

An undercover cop is almost always in danger. Still, he not only has to protect himself, but also his informants. Often the officer is in the company of very unhappy, dangerous people. Some may be on drugs. Many times these people have learned to trust the undercover cop. When they find out they have trusted a police officer, they can get very angry.

An undercover officer must try to control the situation no matter what happens. It's important that he has an escape or backup plan in case of trouble. Working undercover means always thinking ahead about what might happen. It means learning not to panic when things get bad.

Every step a police officer takes must be legal. He has to obey the law at all times. For example, if an undercover cop wants to search

someone's house, he first has to get a warrant (permission from a judge). To get the permission, the officer has to prove probable cause. This means he has good reason to suspect that something illegal is going on.

When making an arrest, the officer has to inform the person about their legal rights. The person under arrest has to know why they are being arrested. They must be told that they have a right to a lawyer. An officer cannot miss even one of these steps. If he does, the case can be dismissed. All the detective's work will be worth nothing.

Dave Macoulian is the made-up name of a real undercover detective. He has one of the most dangerous jobs around. And he knows it. Dave works in the Narcotics Unit of the Baltimore Police Department.

Dave has to be prepared for danger even when he's off-duty. "I'm always armed," he says. "I very rarely go out of the house without a weapon. Not only do I have to protect myself, I have to think about my family, too."

Dave has been investigating drug traffic for eight years. To get into the Narcotics Unit, Dave had to show he could do the work. He had to prove that he was honest. He went through a series of interviews. Then he took drug and lie-detector tests. Dave also had to prove that he could get to know the people dealing drugs. And he had to promise to follow the rules.

Dave's schedule isn't nine to five. He works a lot of odd hours and may not go home for days. Some days he may end up in another state. To work undercover you have to be very patient. "Some cases take a very long time to develop. You can spend a lot of time spinning your wheels," says Dave.

Dave sees a lot of neighborhoods being destroyed because of drugs. "It's amazing," he says. "The drug gangs start moving in and people start moving out. They don't want to confront these people who are obviously dangerous. The whole neighborhood goes down the drain."

Still Dave sees occasional pockets of hope. Neighborhood watch groups and community organizations can sometimes turn a neighborhood around.

Dave's job might seem a tough way to earn a living, but he feels he was probably meant to do it. "Even as a small child, every time a police car would roll by, I'd say: 'That's what I want to do.' There's a lot of people I know who would never want this job. But I love it."

Test Pilot

Early test pilots were daredevils. They often tried to push a plane as far as it could go. It wasn't unusual for them to ditch a number of planes during their careers. Test piloting has changed since then. Today's pilots know a lot more about the planes they are taking into the air. They don't take crazy chances with them. Today's test flyers are sophisticated engineers. Their training costs millions of dollars.

Every new jet fighter and jumbo passenger plane must be tested. The test pilot is responsible for making sure the plane is safe to fly. And he has to make sure it can do the job it is supposed to do.

The first tests of a plane's electronics and computers are done in a simulator. The simulator is a machine that imitates flight. The pilot can try out the controls without leaving the ground. A pilot may spend hundreds of hours in the simulator before he ever gets into the air.

Once airborne, the test pilot's first worries are about the basics of flight. First, the plane needs power. Are the engines working properly? Second, the plane needs to be controlled. Are moving parts, like rudders and flaps, moving the way they should be? Third, the plane needs to be able to take off and land safely. Is the landing gear working properly? Sometimes a first flight only lasts long enough to check out these basic things.

Suppose the plane isn't able to fly safely. The test pilot won't take any chances. If possible, he'll land the aircraft right away. He has a parachute and can eject from the plane in an emergency. But test pilots only do this as a last resort. A new jet fighter costs about 35 million dollars. A jumbo passenger plane can cost twice as much. If it is possible, a test pilot will bring the plane down in one piece.

If a plane's basic tests are all good, the test pilot can move on to trickier tasks. You wouldn't want to be in a 180,000 pound jumbo jet when it stalls, or loses lift. But a test pilot will often make a steep ascent to make a plane do just that. He needs to make sure the aircraft can right itself even if it stalls. Test pilots also shut down and restart engines in midair. Sometimes they may even shut down an

engine on takeoff. This is an especially dangerous thing to do. If the aircraft fails, the pilot is too close to the ground to eject.

Test pilots also land planes in ways that no regular pilot would want to. They come in at dangerous speeds. Or they set down on wet or icy runways. They abort takeoffs, screeching to a stop so quickly that the tires melt. They need to make sure the plane can survive dangerous situations.

Test pilots are very well trained. They have to know how to control an aircraft. They also have to know how to control themselves. The last thing a test pilot can do is panic. He has to know how to ignore his own fear and concentrate on the problem. His life may very well depend on it.

In 1996, for example, an Air Force test pilot for an experimental plane, the X-31, ran into trouble. Karl Lang was returning from a test mission out of Edwards Air Force Base when his plane's controls froze. Though he tried to correct the problem, he wasn't able to save the plane. Lang ditched the X-31 and parachuted to safety.

Even though test pilots follow strict rules, risk is still part of the job.

Kevin Chilton is one of the pilots the U.S. Air Force has trusted to test its aircraft. Chilton was keen to get into the sky ever since he was a kid. He spent hours watching films about flying. "I used to imagine I was really *in* the movie," says Kevin.

At age eleven or twelve, this aspiring pilot got his first ride in a real plane. "I kept asking the pilot: 'Do they really pay you to do this?' I couldn't believe that anyone could get money for doing something so much fun."

At the end of high school, Kevin still wanted to fly, but he couldn't afford the lessons. He decided to enter the Air Force Academy and began to study engineering.

He spent the summers doing research at Edwards Air Force Base in California. Flying with test pilots, Kevin realized that this was the work he wanted to do. Being a test pilot would let him do the two things he loved most: engineering and flying.

After five years of flying for the Air force, Kevin went to test-pilot school for a year. Then he spent two years working as a test pilot.

Kevin's flying proved so successful that he applied to be a NASA astronaut. He has now piloted three successful shuttle missions.

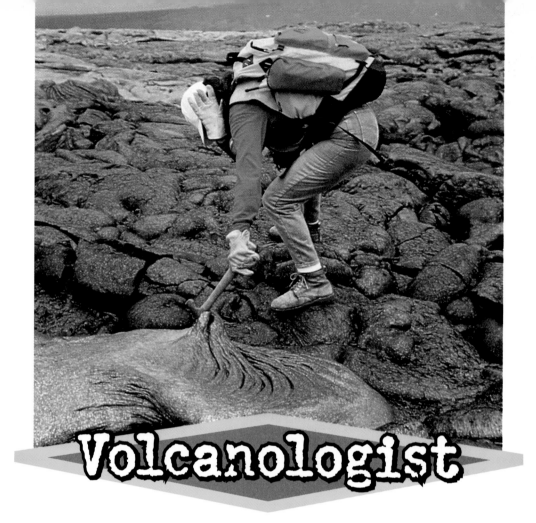

Volcanologist

Volcanoes release the titanic power hidden within the earth. A single eruption can release more energy than thousands of nuclear bombs. One powerful volcano can flatten miles of forests and crush towns and villages.

Figuring out just when a volcano will erupt is an important job. It's also a hard one. Volcanoes are so dangerous because they aren't easy to predict. They often erupt without clear warning.

Volcanologists are scientists who study volcanoes. They look at the earth around and underneath the volcano. They study the gases, ash, and the very hot liquid rock, called lava, coming out of it.

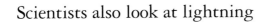

Volcano scientists often use instruments called seismographs. Seismographs show exactly when and how much the earth is moving. Earthquakes often occur underneath volcanoes just before they erupt. Unusual earth-shaking means that a volcano may be ready to blow.

Scientists also look at lightning in the vicinity of a volcano. Often lightning strikes occur in ash clouds when a volcano is erupting.

Instruments are an important part of the volcanologists work. But the scientist also spends time right on top of the volcano. This can mean crawling into a crater bubbling with ponds of steaming lava.

But first he has to get to the volcano. Volcanic mountains are often in far-away places. This can mean some pretty hair-raising work. Volcanologists must sometimes hike through dense rain forests or across shifting ice floes. They have to worry about poisonous snakes and hungry bears. Nearly all volcano scientists carry radios to keep in touch with pilots and their crew.

Once on the mountain, volcano scientists spend time taking

notes. They look at any changes in the volcano's shape and activity. The scientists collect samples of rock and check for fresh lava flows. They are looking for signs that the volcano might erupt.

Back in the lab, the volcano scientist can take a closer look at the samples he's collected. A lot of volcanic rocks just look gray or dark. But a rock can hold a lot of secrets about what is happening inside a volcano. The volcanologist can study the rocks through a magnifying glass. For a closer look, the scientist can cut thin slices of the rock with diamond saws. Then he can look at them through a microscope.

The most dangerous part of a volcanologist's job is being caught in an actual eruption. But the most important readings must be taken when a volcano starts acting up. The scientists warn people ahead of time so they can evacuate. They have to alert emergency services like police, firefighters, and hospital staff. They have to keep ground vehicles and airplanes away from the eruption.

At the same time, the scientist has to be aware of his own safety. Rescuing anyone during a volcanic eruption is almost impossible. An ash cloud can make it difficult to see even a few feet ahead. Eruptions create super-heated winds stronger than a hurricane. If a person doesn't act quickly, there is often no way out.

In his senior year in college, **Steve McNutt** took a course in volcano science. It changed his life. "I was doing a term paper on earthquake activity and volcanoes. I looked for a book on the subject and couldn't find one. I knew then that this is what I wanted to study."

In 1994, Steve went to Colombia in South America to study the Galerus volcano. Scientists believed that Galerus was about to erupt, so it was an excellent time to do research there. On the morning of September 16, Steve joined 11 other researchers on the volcano.

They spent a few hours looking at and climbing into the Galerus crater. Steve collected some rock samples. Then he and half of the other scientists drove back down the mountain. The rest of the scientists stayed to do some more work on the crater. As Steve was driving down the mountain, Galerus erupted. The scientists still at the crater were killed instantly.

Steve had only barely escaped death. Now he had to deal with the loss of friends and fellow workers. It was one of the hardest times of his life. This photo was taken just days after the eruption. Says Steve: "This is probably the saddest I've ever looked."

Bomb Squad Technician

It's hard to think of a job more frightening than working on a bomb squad. Explosive devices can be as big as a truck or as small as a letter. Even the simplest bomb can be deadly. A bomb technician's job is to keep bombs from hurting people.

It all starts with a report of something suspicious. Sometimes a package is left in a public place. No one seems to own it. It has been left for a length of time. When the bomb squad gets the report, they start working on the problem. First, police are sent out to investigate. If they believe there is real danger, they move everyone to a safe place right away. Then they call in the bomb squad.

When the bomb team arrives, they assess the situation. The first thing they must do is make sure everyone is out of the way of a possible blast. Then they go to work.

The technicians have to figure out whether the package is just a package, or something dangerous. To do this they have special tools. They may use listening devices, like stethoscopes, to check for noises inside the package. They can also X-ray it to see what is inside.

If they decide the package is a bomb, they have to make a choice. They can try to disable it right where it is, or they can move it to a safer place.

Moving the bomb to someplace safe is the usual choice. A bomb basket made of lead is put over the item. This will help to confine the blast if the bomb explodes. Then the bomb is put into a containment vessel and taken far away. Other explosives are used to blow it up.

Sometimes, though, a bomb is too risky to move. The bomb squad has to find a way to disable it right where it is. One way is to hose it down with a water cannon. Water can stop parts of the bomb from working and keep it from exploding.

No bomb technician wants to take apart the inside of a bomb. This is the most dangerous work of all. But sometimes it is the only way a bomb can be made safe. To protect themselves, technicians wear special bomb suits. The suits are like bulletproof vests, except they cover the whole body. They carry bomb blankets, too. These can protect the technicians from the full force of a blast.

The bomb team looks for the way a bomb has been set up to explode. This is called the firing train. Figuring this out can be a difficult process. Every minute is dangerous.

If possible, bomb technicians do this work with robots. Some robots are very basic. They can lift or move the bomb. Others are more complicated. They can actually do some of the work of taking the bomb apart. Robots can be moved by cables or by remote control. They allow the technicians to work from a safer distance.

Most bombs that are reported aren't bombs at all. Sometimes they're just hoaxes or fakes. Sometimes they're just innocent packages that people have left behind. But every bomb threat has to be checked out just in case it's real. It may mean the difference between life and death for a lot of people.

Leroy Lucero works for the police department in Santa Fe, New Mexico. Being a bomb technician isn't his only job, but it's one he takes seriously. "You have to accept that it's a very dangerous job," says Leroy.

Every two years Leroy takes a special course about bombs given by the Federal Bureau of Investigation (FBI). He learns about new handling devices for bombs. He also learns about new kinds of explosives.

There are several handling devices that Leroy uses. These include listening devices for hearing inside a container, and bomb baskets and bomb blankets to cover a bomb. He also uses disrupters to stop a bomb from working. All of these items are constantly being updated. "You have to keep up with a fast-changing technology," says the police lieutenant.

Leroy has to stay physically fit for his job. "Otherwise," he says, "you couldn't stand up in a bomb suit. It's made of lead."

The bomb squad in Santa Fe works on about a dozen cases a year. A bomb call-out can involve anything from a suspicious package to a holdup. "Just recently," says Leroy, "a robbery suspect had a bomb. He said he would detonate it unless the money was turned over to him."

Police work has always been part of Leroy's life. "My father was a police officer," says the lieutenant. "I'd always been interested in following in his footsteps. When an opening came up in the bomb squad in 1984, I applied for it. I wanted to do as much as I could for the department."

Leroy thinks there will be more work for bomb squads around the country. "When there is a high profile incident like the one in Oklahoma City, the department gets more calls. We also realize that a bombing can happen anywhere. We have to think: Maybe we're not as safe as we thought we were."

Plague Fighter

The Center for Disease Control (CDC) is in Atlanta, Georgia. This organization tracks down contagious diseases throughout the world. Contagious diseases can spread easily and quickly from person to person. Most of them are caused by extremely tiny organisms called viruses.

When a contagious disease breaks out, CDC field-workers get busy. They go to the place where people are getting sick. They want to identify the virus right away. That way they may stop the disease before many people get ill and die. Usually an epidemic, or outbreak of a disease, has a single starting point. CDC staff work with local doctors. Together they try to locate the first person who got sick with the disease. They want to find the source of the virus or bacteria that causes the sickness.

Sometimes the source is an animal or plant. Workers collect samples of plants and animals that might be infected. Samples are put in sealed containers and shipped back to the laboratory in Atlanta.

Field workers need to locate the origin or cause of the sickness. But finding each and every person who has the disease is also very important. Missing even one case could mean disaster. Contagious diseases can spread through simple touching. Some viruses, called aerosols, can travel quickly through the air. They can be carried in a breath or a sneeze. It's important to contain or limit them as soon as possible.

People who are caring for a sick person can sometimes get sick themselves. CDC workers must wear gloves and plastic masks, and sometimes special suits to protect themselves. Sometimes, after their work is done, they have to burn or destroy their clothing. This keeps the deadly viruses from spreading to other people.

It is important for CDC workers to keep track of any new cases of a disease. They have to do this quickly, otherwise an entire neighborhood could be infected. And they have to make sure that people who might be sick don't travel. They could risk taking the disease to other places.

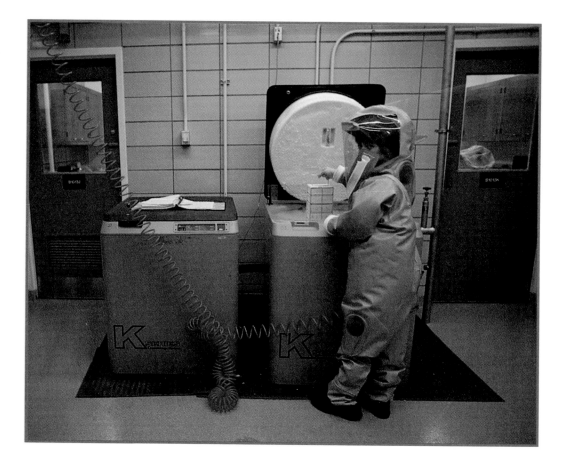

When Marty Monroe goes to work each morning, she puts on something like a space suit. But she isn't getting on a space shuttle. In fact, she isn't going anywhere at all. She puts on the special suit to protect herself.

Marty works in what is called a "hot lab" at the Center for Disease Control. She is an epidemiologist, a person who studies epidemics. Marty works with some of the most deadly viruses in the world. Being completely covered and breathing through a hose helps keep her safe. She is protected from direct contact with dangerous microorganisms. "I feel very secure in the lab," says Marty. "Our walls are eighteen inches thick, and the building is hurricane, tornado, and earthquake proof."

Working in a spacesuit isn't easy. Once inside, Marty can't eat, drink, or even go to the bathroom. "It can get hot inside the suit," says a fellow scientist. "Walking around is hard, too, since the suit weighs twenty pounds."

The suits keep the scientists separated from their samples. The samples Marty looks at are taken from plants and animals in places where deadly epidemics have struck. "A lot of virus samples will just come in the mail from people in different countries," says Marty. "They're packaged in special cans and put on dry ice to make them safe."

Most of Marty's work is done under a microscope. If she can match a sample to a known killer virus, she is in luck. The CDC may be on the road to finding the source of the disease. And they may be able to make a vaccine that will protect people against it. "And," says Marty, "what we learn about one virus may help our work on another. Information about the Ebola virus can help us learn about the measles, for instance."

Marty finds her work exciting. But she also cautions people against being too scared about outbreaks. "Although these viruses sound scary," she says, "not many people get sick from them. Many more people die from accidents and common diseases."

Skywalker

High above the sidewalks of Manhattan are some true acrobats. Their circus acts aren't done on a high wire, but on steel beams. They are the skywalkers of the construction industry. For them, a stroll across a beam, forty stories up, is just a days work.

Around the turn of the twentieth century, buildings started getting taller. Bridges started getting longer and wider. All of these structures relied on steel beams linked together. They needed a strong skeleton to hold them up.

Special people were needed to work on these high steel structures.

Walking without a net across a steel beam forty floors up takes special courage. Keeping your feet on the beam when a gale is blowing takes even more. Many regular construction workers refused to work on high bridges and skyscrapers. In fact, most of the original skywalkers were Mohawk and other Iroquois. These Indians had little or no fear of walking across the beams at great heights.

Courage alone, though, doesn't make a skywalker. High steelworkers must be on guard against falling. But they also have to be aware of the workers around them. Falling steel beams can injure or kill a steelworker in an instant. Spotting danger before something bad happens is important. Showing off can get you killed.

Today many skyscrapers no longer use steel structures. Instead they use cast concrete. But that doesn't mean the job of high steelworkers has disappeared. Today, many have become rodmen. Rodmen tie steel rods, called rebar, together. Rebar is used to reinforce the concrete. These workers have to remember all the different sizes of the steel bars. They have to know how to tie them together. A rodman ties about one ton of steel every day, always with his feet high off the ground.

Modern high steelworkers don't just put buildings up. They also take them down, especially structures like bridges. In these cases all the work has to be done in reverse. This kind of work is twice as dangerous. A weakened building can easily come apart while workers are on it. A high steelworker has to overcome his natural fears. At the same time, he has to trust his feel for the level of danger. Sometimes a situation is just too dangerous to keep working. A good skywalker will know when the risk of injury is too great.

Mike Bomberry grew up on the Six Nations Indian Reservation in Ontario, Canada. At fifteen and a half, Mike quit school. Not long after this, his dad made him get a job. "My father said: 'If you're not going to go to school, you're going to go to work.'"

From that point on Mike traveled. He worked his way across the United States as a skywalker. He traveled to California, Washington, Texas, and Louisiana. Wherever the work was, that's where Mike would be. He straddled the high beams in every season. "I never minded the weather," says Mike. "Sometimes it dropped to twenty-six degrees below zero and sometimes it would stay over one hundred degrees for weeks. We worked through all of it."

Mike hasn't only worked at putting buildings up. He has also taken them down. Pulling down a bridge in Pittsburgh, Pennsylvania, his crew got a rude shock. The bridge shifted and the steel supports began to break. Mike came out fine that time. But a few years ago he broke four ribs when a steel beam rolled over onto him. The weight of it sent him crashing through the floor of a building.

That wasn't Mike's most dramatic skywalking experience. Working in New York City several years ago, a gust of wind caught a beam he was on. It swung it out away from the building. Mike was hanging from a steel bar ten stories up over a busy Manhattan street!

Today Occupational Safety and Health Administration (OSHA) regulations restrict high steelwork. Skywalkers can't do some of the more dangerous things they used to do on high buildings. The regulations have taken some of the danger out of the job. Some of the thrills are gone, too. But for high steelworkers, the essential satisfaction is still there. They can still see the triumphant result of something their hands have built.

Index

ABOUT THE AUTHOR

June A. English has a knack for finding people with unusual jobs. During her career she has interviewed demolition experts, alligator scientists, and trapeze artists. Her other books for Scholastic include the *Encyclopedia of Transportation* and *Mission: Earth* (with NASA astronaut Thomas D. Jones).